D0633168

2 5/11

SPACE!

THE SUN

GEORGE CAPACCIO

Marshall Cavendish
Benchmark
New York

Marshall Cavendish Benchmark
99 White Plains Road
Tarrytown, New York 10591
www.marshallcavendish.us

Library of Congress Cataloging-in-Publication Data

Capaccio, George.
    The sun / by George Capaccio.
        p. cm. -- (Space!)
    Summary: "Describes the Sun, including its history, its composition, and its role in the
    solar system"--Provided by publisher.
    Includes bibliographical references and index.
    ISBN 978-07614-4242-4
    1. Sun--Juvenile literature. I. Title.
    QB5215.C366 2010
    5237--dc22
2008037275

Editor: Karen Ang
Publisher: Michelle Bisson
Art Director: Anahid Hamparian
Series Design by Daniel Roode
Production by nSight, Inc.

Front cover: A computer illustration of the Sun
Title page: The HESSI spacecraft was sent into outer space to collect information
    about solar flares.
Photo research by Candlepants, Incorporated
Front cover: Detlev van Ravenswaay / Photo Researchers Inc.
The photographs in this book are used by permission and through the courtesy
of: NASA: Spectrum Astro Inc., 1, 55; NASA, ESA, N. Smith (University of California,
Berkeley), and The Hubble Heritage Team, 31; 45, 48; JPL, 53; NASA, ESA, K.Noll,/ The
Hubble Heritage Team, 57. Getty Images: Ian Mckinnell, 4; Art Montes De Oca, 36;
Travelpix Ltd, 42, 43; Keren Su, 44; Peter Cade, 46; Steven Nourse, 49; AFP, 50. Super Stock:
Pixtal, 7, 32, 58; Digital Vision Ltd., 13. Photo Researchers Inc.: Gerard Lodriguss, 10;
Gianni Tortoli, 20; David Nicholls, 24; Mark Garlick, 47. Art Resource, NY: James Morris,
14, 15; Erich Lessing, 16; Edward Owen, 18; Image Select, 23. SOHO (ESA & NASA): 34, 38,
39, 40, 41; 26, 27, 51, 54.
Printed in Malaysia
123456

CONTENTS

1

SPACE

Have you ever looked up at the night sky and wondered about outer space, or tried to imagine how big the universe is? Does it go on forever? How did it come to be? What is it made of? These are the kinds of questions that **astronomers**—people who study space—have long been trying to answer. Over the last several centuries, science has taught us a great deal about the structure of space and the origin of the universe. But space is still a place of wonder and mystery with so many secrets waiting to be uncovered.

Earth is surrounded by an atmosphere composed of gases— almost 79 percent nitrogen, just under 21 percent oxygen, and 1 percent other gases. All of these gases together make up the air

The universe extends far beyond what we can see—even with special telescopes and spacecraft. Advanced technologies and new discoveries have taught us more about outer space, but much of it still remains a mystery.

5

we breathe. The higher we go above the surface of Earth the less air there is to breathe. At about 250 miles (400 kilometers) from the surface of Earth, there is almost no air at all. A **vacuum** is a place without air, and outer space is a vacuum.

Outer space has extreme temperatures, too. In places where there is no sunlight, the temperature can come very close to absolute zero, which is -459 degrees Fahrenheit (-273 degrees Celsius). The coldest temperature ever recorded on Earth was -129 degrees Fahrenheit (-89 degrees C) in Antarctica. So outer space is much, much colder. But when sunlight or some other heat source is present, the temperature in parts of outer space can reach 250 degrees Fahrenheit (120 degrees C). That is about twice as hot as California's Death Valley on an extremely hot day.

THE UNIVERSE

Before the age of manned spacecraft and orbiting **satellites**, people thought the universe was unchanging. It had no beginning and no end. Even Albert Einstein, one of the greatest physicists and mathematicians of all time, decided the universe never changes. He believed it would stay the same size forever, without expanding or contracting. By the beginning of the twentieth century, most astronomers also had a very limited idea about the size of the universe. They believed our own galaxy, the Milky Way, was the whole universe. In 1910 Harlow

The light from stars that twinkle in the night sky travels millions of miles before it reaches us. The star closest to Earth—the Sun—is around 93 million miles away.

Shapley, an American astronomer, determined that the Milky Way measures about 100,000 light years across. One light year is the distance light travels in a year. Since the speed of light is 186,000 miles per second (300,000 km per second), then one light year is 186,000 miles/second x 60 seconds/minute x 60 minutes/ hour x 24 hours/day x 365 days/year = 5,865,696,000,000 miles/ year (9,460,800,000,000 km/year). So 100,000 light years is about 600,000 trillion miles!

But in the 1920s Edwin Hubble, another American astronomer, pushed our understanding of the universe further than it had

7

ever been before. Using what was then the largest and most powerful telescope in the world, Hubble detected enormous galaxies beyond the Milky Way. But even more far-reaching was his discovery that these galaxies were all moving away from our own at an incredible speed. Could the universe be expanding outward, moving away from some central point? If this were the case, then the universe must have had a definite beginning in the very distant past. But how did the universe begin? What caused it to start expanding?

THE BIG BANG

Today, most scientists accept the Big Bang theory as our most reliable model of how the universe began. This theory maintains that the universe began between 12 and 14 billion years ago. Long before there were stars, galaxies, planets, or solar systems, the universe existed as a hot, dense mass about the size of a pebble or a coin. But then it began to expand and has continued to do so. Over billions of years, the universe has evolved into a vast, star-studded place where galaxies blossom like fireworks and stars are born and die.

Scientists revise the Big Bang theory as more information becomes available from space missions, telescopes, and computer models. For example, scientists now think that the Big Bang was not actually an explosion that took place at a central point in space. When the universe was born, space was born, too. And space appeared everywhere at the same time. One way to understand this is to imagine someone blowing up a basketball. Imagine that the surface of the ball stands for the universe. As the ball is filled with air, the surface spreads out. All points on the surface are moving away from each other as the ball expands, just all points in space expand as the universe expands.

Edwin Hubble's amazing discovery of galaxies in motion was the first visible evidence in support of the Big Bang theory. But more evidence was to come. In 1964, two other scientists detected what they believed was the afterglow of the Big Bang. Imagine the glowing embers from a campfire that has stopped burning. The afterglow of the Big Bang is like those embers, only on a cosmic scale. It fills the universe and is called **cosmic microwave background radiation (CMB)**. We cannot actually see it because our eyes do not see **microwaves**. But if we could, then we would see the entire sky glowing brightly everywhere we looked.

Of course, after so many billions of years, the universe has had plenty of time to cool off since its super hot beginning. No place on Earth ever gets as cold as the coldest temperatures in outer space. But even there the temperature never drops to absolute zero. Because the leftover heat from the Big Bang is evenly spread out, the temperature in space will always be about

These stargazers use their telescopes to look at the Milky Way on a summer night.

2.73 degrees above absolute zero. The presence of this heat, or cosmic microwave background radiation, is strong evidence that the Big Bang happened.

GALAXIES AND STARS

In a tiny fraction of a second after the Big Bang, the universe did something almost impossible to imagine. With extraordinary speed, it swelled from the size of a pebble to a vast but mostly empty space. At first, the only matter that existed was tiny subatomic particles. There were still no stars, galaxies, or planets. As the universe continued to expand and cool, these particles combined to form molecules of hydrogen, helium, and lithium. Over millions of years, larger and larger forms of matter were created as more and more molecules bonded together. This process eventually led to the formation of stars and galaxies.

Galaxies

Think of what happens when warm air inside a car comes into contact with cold air outside—drops of water form on the car's windows, which is called condensation. Similarly, as the incredibly hot early universe cooled, matter slowly began to condense. And from these enormous condensations of matter came the first galaxies. Galaxies are the largest objects in the universe. Basically, a galaxy is a cluster of stars, dust, and gas held together by the force of **gravity**. Galaxies range in size from a few thousand to a million light years in diameter.

In 2004 the Hubble Space Telescope, which is based in outer space, captured light from the oldest galaxies in the universe. Scientists estimate that these galaxies began to form anywhere from 400 to 800 million years after the Big Bang. To see these galaxies you would have to go back in time billions of years—almost to the birth of the universe itself.

Our own galaxy is a **spiral galaxy** called the Milky Way. It contains about 100 billion stars and extends about 100,000 light years across. The Milky Way's center is roughly 10,000 light years

TYPES OF GALAXIES

Astronomers classify galaxies according to their shape. Spiral galaxies look like pinwheels. They have arms that spiral outward as the entire galaxy rotates. Spirals generally have more middle-aged stars. Elliptical galaxies contain mostly older stars and resemble stretched circles. A small percentage of galaxies cannot be easily classified. These are called irregular galaxies. They are mostly made up of young stars.

thick and may contain a massive **black hole**. Because the Milky Way is so huge, we are not able to get outside of it to see exactly what it looks like. However, scientists agree that it probably resembles the Andromeda Galaxy, our nearest neighbor, which is about 2.5 million light years from Earth.

Our galaxy is called the Milky Way because part of it forms a long, whitish band of light. Like other spiral galaxies, the Milky Way has three distinct regions: a bulge, a halo, and a disk. The bulge, or center, contains mostly older stars and very little gas or dust. The halo is the home of groups of stars called globular clusters. Each cluster contains hundreds of thousands of stars. The disk is a kind of stellar nursery where new stars are constantly forming.

Stars

Stars come in a variety of sizes and colors. The color of a star is an indication of its surface temperature. The hottest stars are blue. The next hottest are white. The coolest are yellow, orange, and red. Stars range in size from small **white dwarfs** to super giants. Giant stars are extremely bright but they have a low surface temperature. The brightness or **luminosity** of a star is a measure of how much energy it is generating. A star shines because it is burning huge amounts of hydrogen in non-stop nuclear reactions.

Our Sun is an average-sized star. It is located about 26,000 light years from the center of the Milky Way, along one of the spiral arms of our galaxy. The Sun is also the hub—or center—of the solar system, which includes Earth and seven other planets. It takes about 200 million years for the Sun to complete its orbit around the center of the Milky Way. In astronomical time, one orbit of the Sun is equal to one cosmic year. One cosmic year ago on Earth, dinosaurs were still walking around!

Though we see the sun as a bright ball of orange, white, yellow, and red, the Sun is actually classified as a yellow star.

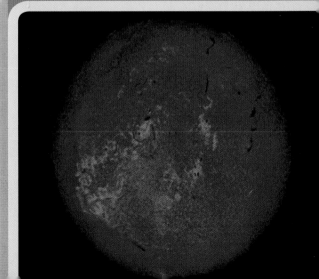

2

EARLY THEORIES ABOUT THE SUN

Early humans could not have imagined what makes the Sun shine or how it came to be. But they knew from daily experience that without the Sun there would be no life on Earth. To express their sense of the Sun's importance, they created stories. Some of these stories have survived thousands of years of human history. Today we think of them as myths. Sun myths tell us a great deal about what ancient cultures thought about the Sun. The stories themselves are often imaginative explanations of the Sun's origin and nature.

The ancient Egyptians, for instance, worshipped the Sun as a god whom they called Ra. In Egyptian carvings and paintings, Ra is often pictured as a man with the head of a hawk or falcon.

An ancient painting on the wall of an Egyptian tomb shows the Sun god Ra. The large disk on his head is his crown that represents the Sun.

THE SUN

For a crown, he wears a large disk representing the Sun. The Egyptians believed the actual Sun was either Ra's eye or his entire body. They imagined that each morning Ra set out on a day-long journey across the sky in a marvelous boat. At night, he returned home in a different boat. He had to travel through a mysterious underworld where various monsters tried to destroy him. Fortunately, Ra was always victorious, so each new morning he was able to resume his journey across the sky and bring light and warmth to the world.

The ancient Greeks, like the Egyptians, thought of the Sun as a powerful god. The Greeks called him Helios. For them, Helios was a young man who rode from east to west in a golden chariot pulled by four flaming horses. The horses had wings and may have stood for the four seasons. At the end of the day, Helios loaded his chariot and his horses into a giant cup or bowl. Then he sailed home on a mythical river that was supposed to circle the world. In the morning, Helios would begin his journey all over again, rising up in the east with his horses leading the way.

The ancient Greeks believed that Helios drove his golden chariot from east to west because the Sun rose in the east and set in the west.

16

Native American cultures have their own fascinating stories about the Sun and how it came to be. Pacific Coast tribes in North America tell of the time when the world was always dark and cold. There was no light except from the Moon and stars. But then one day Raven saw something glowing in the distance. He flew toward this brightness and discovered that it came from a yellow ball. The ball was kept in a locked box. But Raven tricked the owners of the ball and took it back to his people. He placed it in the sky where it continues to shine. That yellow ball, of course, was the Sun.

SEEING THE SUN IN A NEW LIGHT

At one time, most people believed that Earth was the center of the solar system. According to this view, the Sun and the rest of the planets all revolve around Earth. Of course, it is not too hard to imagine why people once thought this way. After all, the Sun seems to rise in the east and set in the west. And if this is the case, then the Sun must be traveling across the sky and making a complete orbit around Earth every day.

Almost two thousand years ago, an astronomer named Ptolemy expressed this Earth-centered view of the solar system in mathematical terms. Ptolemy lived in Egypt in the city of

This illustration shows the Ptolemaic view of the solar system, in which all planets, moons, and stars orbit Earth.

Alexandria. Since telescopes still had not been invented, he had to rely on his own observations as well as on the work of earlier scientists. In Ptolemy's view, Earth was fixed—or in one place—in space. It did not move. Instead, the Sun and the five known planets moved around the Earth. Ptolemy used geometric formulas to describe their orbits, which he thought of as perfect circles.

Ptolemy's model of the solar system remained unchallenged for more than a thousand years. Then, in the sixteenth century, a Polish astronomer named Nicolaus Copernicus concluded that Ptolemy—and all the ancient Greek astronomers whose work had inspired him—were wrong. According to Copernicus, Earth was not the center of the solar system. The Sun was the center, and all the planets, including Earth, revolved around it. Copernicus also argued that Earth made one complete rotation every day and took one year to travel around the Sun.

18

Five hundred years ago, these were totally new ideas to most people. They challenged the everyday observation that the Sun appeared to revolve around Earth, which seemed to stay in one place. And they threatened people's sense of who they were and what it meant to be human. If Earth was just one more planet orbiting the Sun, then maybe humans were not all that special either.

Copernicus knew how dangerous his ideas were. He only shared them with a few of his fellow astronomers. Toward the end of his life, Copernicus finally agreed to have his work published as a book for the entire world to see. Unfortunately, he never saw the printed book because he died before it came out. Its publication marks a major turning point in the development of science. The book's Sun-centered view of the solar system changed forever our view of ourselves and our place in the universe.

GALILEO TAKES A CLOSER LOOK

The next major advance in the study of the Sun did not happen until nearly seventy years after Copernicus' death. In 1609 an Italian astronomer, Galileo Galilei, heard about a man in Holland who had invented a new device called a spyglass. A long tube with a lens at each end, it made faraway objects appear close up. Inspired by news of this invention, Galileo began working on his own spyglass. He shaped his own lenses and kept on improving their magnifying power. Eventually, his spyglass, or telescope, could take in about fifty-five times more light than the human eye and could enlarge objects about twenty times. Galileo's use of a telescope meant the Sun could now become an object of scientific study for the first time in history.

Galileo used this telescope to gaze in outer spac where he discovered the planet Jupiter.

When Galileo turned this simple telescope toward the night sky, he made a series of astounding discoveries. He saw craters and mountains on the surface of our Moon, detected four moons orbiting the planet Jupiter, and charted Venus's orbit around the

Sun. These and other discoveries convinced Galileo that Nicolaus Copernicus had been right: the Sun was the center of the solar system, not Earth. But even in Galileo's day most people still did not accept this view. They still believed that Earth was the center of the entire universe and all the other heavenly bodies must be perfect in every way.

With his telescope, Galileo began investigating dark patches on the face of the Sun. Other observers, also using a telescope, studied these **sunspots**. Christoph Scheiner, a German scientist, thought they were small planets circling the Sun. Scheiner refused to believe that the Sun had spots and might not be perfect. Galileo's observations, however, proved that the dark areas were actually features of the Sun's surface. We now know that Galileo was correct. Sunspots are areas on the Sun that are cooler than the Sun's normal surface temperature. Because they are cooler, they appear as dark spots.

Galileo's open support for the ideas of Nicolaus Copernicus got him into serious trouble. The religious authorities of his day wanted everyone to accept an Earth-centered view of the universe. But Galileo's scientific observations had shown him this view was completely false. When he published a book in favor of the Copernican model, those authorities accused him of going against the teachings of the Church. Galileo was sentenced to house arrest for the rest of his life.

ISAAC NEWTON AND THE COLORS OF LIGHT

In 1642 Galileo died in his home outside of Florence, Italy. That same year one of the greatest scientific minds of all time was born. His name was Isaac Newton, and he was born in England. When he was in his twenties, Newton began experimenting with prisms, which are carefully cut pieces of glass. He placed one prism in a beam of sunlight entering his room. The sunlight passed through the glass and created a stunning rainbow, or color spectrum. It was common knowledge that prisms could create a rainbow effect. But people thought the prisms somehow added color to the light. Newton wanted to prove that sunlight itself contained all the colors of the rainbow. When he placed a second prism upside down in front of the first, the colors recombined to form pure, white light. His experiment was a success. He had shown that white light is composed of the colors red, orange, yellow, green, blue, violet, and purple.

Newton's discovery led other scientists to study the color spectrum not only of sunlight but also of different chemical elements. By the middle of the nineteenth century, astronomers could tell what gases and other substances are found in the Sun and even more distant stars. They did this with the aid of an instrument called a spectroscope. A spectroscope reveals

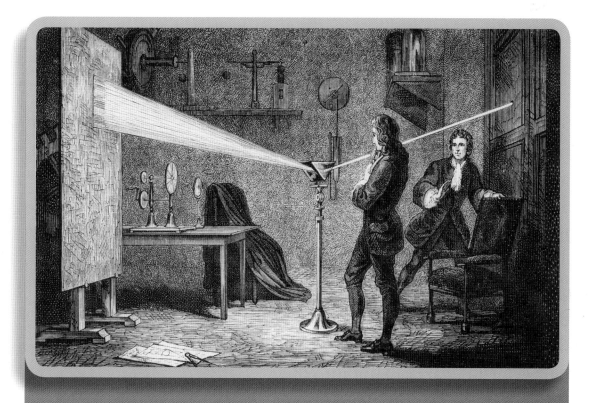

Sir Isaac Newton was famous for many of his scientific discoveries, but one of the earliest involved using prisms to show that sunlight contained all the colors of the rainbow.

the colors that make up sunlight as well as light from heated elements. By studying the colors, astronomers can then identify the elements since each element has its own unique color spectrum. That is how helium was discovered. It turned up as a yellow line in a color spectrum of sunlight. We now know that this gas makes up about 25 percent of the Sun.

ELEMENTARY PARTICLES POINT THE WAY

Spectroscopy, or the study of color spectra (which is plural for "spectrum"), allowed scientists to figure out what the Sun is made of. But how does the Sun produce so much energy? That was a question that baffled scientists for many years. The answer depended on groundbreaking discoveries in the field of physics. In the twentieth century, physicists like Albert Einstein and Ernest Rutherford began looking into the subatomic world of **elementary particles**. These are the building blocks of all matter. The most common ones are protons, neutrons, and electrons. The discovery of elementary particles led to the discovery of nuclear fusion. When nuclear fusion occurs, two or more atoms are fused, or bound, together. In the process, a great amount of energy is released.

Atoms are made up of three different subatomic, or elementary, particles: protons, neutrons, and electrons. Protons and neutrons are found inside the nucleus, or center, of the atom, while electrons orbit the nucleus.

24

In 1938 two physicists, Hans Bethe and Charles Critchfield, showed how the centers, or nuclei, of hydrogen joined to create helium nuclei. This type of nuclear fusion, they said, takes place deep in the core of all stars, including our Sun. In other words, the Sun shines because it is constantly converting hydrogen into helium through the process of nuclear fusion. The Sun is like a giant thermonuclear reactor!

In order to shine, the Sun has to keep its nuclear fires burning. Astronomers calculate that since its birth, the Sun has been converting about 700 billion tons of hydrogen into helium and light every second! The Sun has so much hydrogen that it has taken about 4.5 billion years to use up half of its supply. So how long will it take to use up the remainder of its hydrogen? If you guessed another 4.5 billion years, you would be right.

Understanding what the Sun is made of and how it generates energy is not the end of the story. The study of the Sun, or solar science, has come a long, long way since Ptolemy in the first century. But many questions remain.

Today, orbiting spacecraft and powerful Earth-based observatories allow astronomers to look deeply into the Sun and other stars. Supercomputers analyze data from satellites and telescopes and use this information to create models of the Sun's features. In the future we may finally understand all the mysteries of our closest star, the Sun.

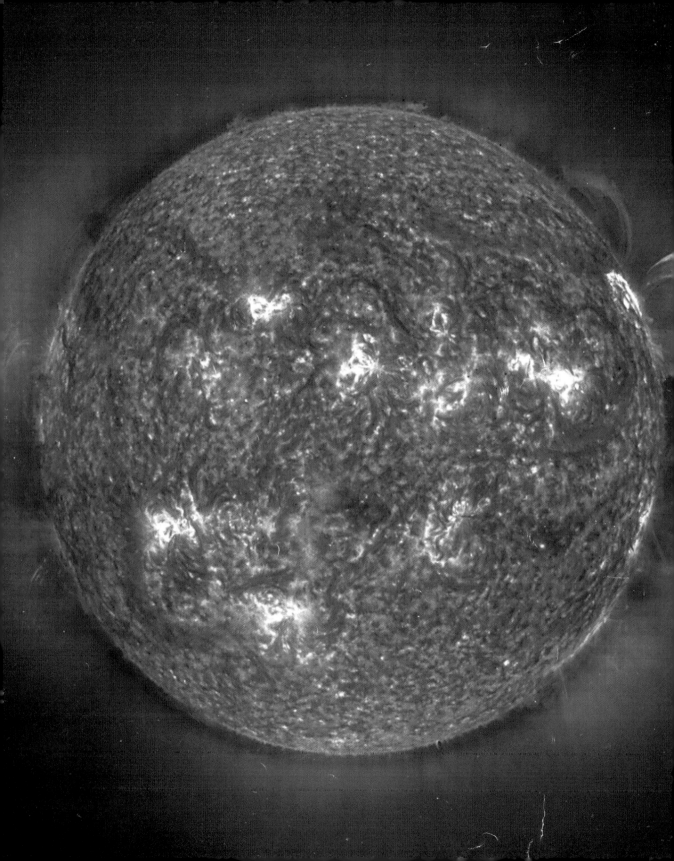

3

STRUCTURE AND PHYSICAL FEATURES OF THE SUN

A STAR AMONG STARS

Our Sun is a star. It is one of approximately 100 billion stars in the Milky Way galaxy. As stars go, our Sun is pretty average. There are other stars that are much bigger and brighter, and stars that are smaller and not nearly as bright as the Sun. But for an average star, our Sun is really, really big. Its diameter is about 860,000 miles (1.4 million km). It would take more than one hundred Earths, lined up side by side, to cover this distance.

This image of the Sun displays the different levels of heat found throughout this burning star. The whitish areas are much hotter than the darker red areas.

THE SUN

If the Sun were a huge hollow ball, it would take more than a million Earths to fill it.

Fortunately, the Sun is not too far away and not too close, either. At a comfortable distance of 93 million miles (150 million km), it provides us with all the light and warmth we need in order to live. So just how hot is the Sun? Temperatures in the Sun's core reach more than 28 million degrees Fahrenheit (15.5 million degrees C). But the surface temperature is much, much cooler—about 10,000 degrees Fahrenheit (5500 degrees C). Beyond the surface, temperatures start rising again.

The Sun's atmosphere, which extends for millions of miles into space, can reach more than 1 million degrees Fahrenheit (555,538 degrees C). Scientists are still trying to understand why temperatures further from the surface are so much hotter.

The Sun, like most average-size stars, is a burning, churning, spinning sphere of hydrogen, helium, and other gases. It is not solid like the Earth. On the other hand, it is not a flaming ball of gas, either. No spacecraft has come close enough to take samples of the Sun. But thanks to high-powered telescopes, scientists now think the gases that make up the Sun exist as plasmas. The three most common forms of matter are solids, liquids, and gases. Plasmas are a fourth and very mysterious form of matter. Everyday examples of plasmas on Earth include lightning, fluorescent lights, and neon signs. You may even have seen a plasma ball on display in a science center. A gas can

Eight major planets and the dwarf planet Pluto orbit around the Sun. Each planet's distance from the Sun and the shape of its orbit determine many of the planet's characteristics.

become plasma when it is highly charged or energized. In the Sun, extremely high temperatures energize solar gases and turn them into plasmas.

The Sun is the largest object in our solar system, which includes eight orbiting planets, asteroids, and comets, and the dwarf planet Pluto. (Pluto had once been classified as a planet, but because of its small size, scientists now consider it a dwarf planet.) The Sun is so large it accounts for more than 99 percent of the total mass in the solar system. Without the Sun's powerful gravitational force, the solar system would collapse and cease to exist. And of course, without the Sun's continuous outpouring of light and heat, life on Earth would be impossible.

HOW WAS THE SUN CREATED?

The short answer to this question is that the Sun, like all stars, began as a dense cloud of interstellar gas and dust. The long answer takes us back to Isaac Newton. Experimenting with prisms was only a very small part of Newton's scientific work. Later on in his career, he came up with a set of laws that account for the behavior of all matter in the universe. One of his laws—the Law of Gravity—states that objects naturally attract each other.

An old story says that Newton was sitting under an apple tree on his mother's farm when an apple bounced off his head. At that moment, he had what we would now call a "brainstorm," or moment of inspiration. According to this legend, Newton suddenly realized that gravity is the force that attracts one object to another. Actually, the story is not true—at least the part about an apple falling on his head. But Newton did wonder about attracting forces. Is the force that pulls all objects downward the same force that keeps the Moon orbiting around the Earth? After making a series of calculations, Newton decided the two forces were one and the same. He named this force gravity. Thanks to Newton's insights, we now know that the power of gravity is what made the birth of the Sun possible.

Astronomers estimate that the Sun is about 4.5 billion years old. By studying the way other stars are born, they have come up with a reasonable explanation for how the Sun was created. For starters, imagine a time billions of years ago when there was no Sun. Where a brilliant star would one day shine, there only

By observing the behavior of other nebulae, such as the Carina Nebula, scientists can figure out how stars and solar systems are formed.

existed a **nebula** of dust and gas in the vacuum of space. This cloud was not the sort of cloud we see floating across the sky. It was millions of miles wide. Instead of containing moisture like clouds on Earth, it was made of molecules of gas and grains of dust.

According to Newton's Law of Gravity, all these molecules and grains should have squeezed together and become compressed. But they did not because they were too spread out for gravity to kick in. Newton recognized that the smaller the distance between objects, the greater the attraction. The opposite is also true—the greater the distance, the weaker the attraction. Something was needed to compress the cloud and bring the particles closer together. Only then would gravity take over and start the process of star formation.

Astronomers theorize that this "something" was a **supernova**. A supernova is what happens when a giant red star explodes. The blast wave from such a tremendous explosion could have plowed into the cold cloud of dust and molecules. As the distance

Supernova explosions are not common in our own galaxy, but scientists are able to observe such explosions in neighboring galaxies.

between the particles decreased, the force of gravity increased. As a result, the cloud began to collapse on itself. But something else also happened. The particles began to interact more violently the closer they came to each other. This is another way of saying that the internal temperature of the nebula increased. (Temperature is actually a measure of how fast atoms are moving. The higher the temperature, the faster the movement.)

A powerful event like a supernova could have caused the nebula to begin contracting. For a period of 100 to 200 million years, it continued to contract, drawing gas molecules and other particles closer and closer together. The center of the cloud became a hub around which the cloud began to circulate. Imagine a figure skater spinning in place on the ice. As the skater brings his or her arms close to the sides of the body, the skater spins faster and faster. Similarly, as the more distant portions of the cloud contracted toward the center, the cloud spun faster and faster, taking the shape of a spinning disk. By this point, the cloud had become a rich environment in which the Sun and all the planets were slowly growing.

Eventually, the temperatures in the center of the cloud became so hot that atoms of hydrogen began to fuse together. These thermonuclear reactions produced the element helium and released a large amount of energy in the form of heat and light. The heat created an outward pressure that worked against the inward pull of gravity. The fiery nucleus of the nebula slowly stopped contracting. It had become a stable, independent source of energy. In other words, it had become a star. This star—our Sun—has been shining steadily ever since.

THE STRUCTURE OF THE SUN

Since landing on the Sun is not possible, astronomers have had to rely on computer models and telescopic observations when studying it. From this ongoing work has come a reliable picture of the Sun's structure.

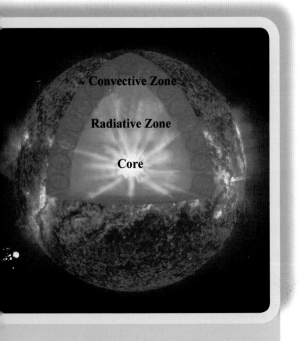

Processes in each of the three layers, or zones, of the Sun work together to convert the thermonuclear reactions into heat and light.

Scientists now know that the Sun's interior has three major layers or zones. The innermost layer is the **solar core**. The core is the powerhouse of the Sun. This is where thermonuclear reactions convert about 700 billion tons of hydrogen into helium every second. These reactions release an incredible amount of energy. Through a very complex process, this energy eventually reaches the surface of the Sun and from there radiates throughout the entire solar system. On Earth we experience this energy as warmth and light, or sunshine.

Moving outward from the core, the next layer is the radiative zone. Energy from the core takes hundreds of thousands of years to travel through the radiative zone. Why does it take so long? Even though this **radiation** is traveling at the speed of light, it has to zigzag through very dense plasma, which greatly slows down its passage.

Above the radiative zone is the convection zone. The temperature drops from about 3.6 million degrees Fahrenheit (2 million degrees C) to around 10,000 degrees Fahrenheit (5700 degrees C). A process known as **convection** carries the energy. Have you ever watched a pot of boiling water on the stove? Gas bubbles carry the heat from the stove's burner to the surface of the water. A similar process takes place in the convection zone as bubbles of hot plasma rise toward the Sun's surface and cooler plasma sinks. This rising and falling creates currents that carry the energy upward. In the convection zone the energy travels much faster than it did in the radiative zone. By the time it reaches the surface, the energy is mostly in the form of visible light.

The Sun's atmosphere consists of three distinct regions: the **photosphere**, the **chromosphere**, and the **corona**. The photosphere is the visible surface of the Sun—the part we can see from Earth. It is only about 62 miles (100 km) thick. The photosphere looks smooth to the naked eye. But close-up images show that it is actually very bumpy. The bumps, called granules, are short-lived bubbles of hot gas that only last a few minutes. As one granule dissolves, another one takes its place. A granule's diameter ranges from 186 to 994 miles (300 to 1,600 km). So an average-size granule is almost as wide as the state of Texas!

Above the photosphere are the chromosphere and the corona. The chromosphere is only visible with the help of special instruments or during a solar eclipse when the Moon comes between the Sun and Earth. When the Moon blocks out light from the much brighter photosphere, we can see the orange-red color of the Sun's chromosphere. Oddly enough, areas farther from the surface of the Sun have higher temperatures. In the chromosphere, the average temperature is about 36,000 degrees Fahrenheit (20,000 degrees C). This layer is between 1,000 and 2,000 miles (1,609 and 3,218 km) thick.

The outermost layer of the Sun's atmosphere is the corona. It extends for millions of miles into space. The corona is the hottest part of the Sun's atmosphere with temperatures as high as 1.8 million degrees Fahrenheit (1 million degrees C). It consists of superheated gases, or plasma, escaping

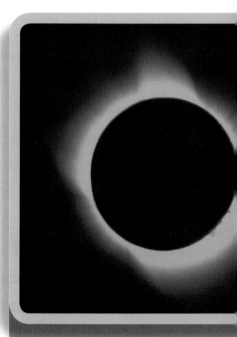

The Sun's chromosphere can be seen during a solar eclipse, when the Moon blocks out the photosphere. In this photograph, the dark area is the Moon and the bright light around it is the Sun's chromosphere.

into outer space. Astronomers have only recently begun to understand why temperatures in the corona are so much higher than they are closer to the Sun's surface.

SOLAR WIND, SUNSPOTS, AND FLARES

For a middle-aged star, our Sun is a mighty dynamo. During every second of its life it cranks out trillions of megawatts of light. It also releases a high-speed wind that blows across the solar system. This wind is not like the wind we experience on Earth. It is a steady stream of subatomic particles pouring off the Sun's corona. The **solar wind** is similar to steam from a pot of boiling water. But instead of water vapor, the solar wind is composed of highly charged electrons and protons. These particles whiz through space at dizzying speeds between 280 miles and 1,056 miles (450 km and 1,700 km) per second. The average speed of the solar wind is 1 million miles per hour (1.6 million km per hour)! The solar wind can cause dramatic effects on Earth as well as interfere with the flight paths of spacecraft. Solar wind is able to shape the magnetic fields around the planets and bend the tails of comets away from the Sun.

Scientists are now thinking about using the solar wind to propel spacecraft beyond our solar system. In 2010 the first interstellar probe spacecraft will unfurl a large solar sail in space. Possibly made of carbon fibers, this high-tech sail will use the power of sunlight the same way conventional sails use the wind. Best of all, unlike rockets, spacecraft with solar sails will require less fuel!

The charged particles in solar winds travel millions of miles before they reach Earth's atmosphere.

Sunspots look like dark patches on the surface of the Sun. The largest sunspots, with diameters between 25,000 and 30,000 miles (40,225 and 48,270 km), are several times bigger than the Earth, which has a diameter of close to 8,000 miles (12,872 km) at the Equator. Sunspots appear dark because they are cooler than the surrounding photosphere. Therefore, they release less light.

Astronomers have been studying sunspots for centuries. Almost three thousand years ago, the Chinese gave the world the first written record of sunspots. These ancient astronomers believed that sunspots were omens that foretold the future. In the seventeenth century, Galileo was one of the first European astronomers to observe sunspots through a telescope. Since then, continuous observations have shown that the number of sunspots goes up and down over an eleven-year cycle. The solar maximum is that point in the cycle when the Sun has the largest number of sunspots. It is also the time when the Sun is most active.

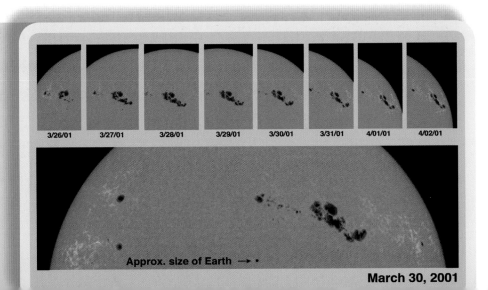

This series of photographs taken in 2001 charted the movement of sunspots as the Sun rotated during a solar cycle.

3/26/01 3/27/01 3/28/01 3/29/01 3/30/01 3/31/01 4/01/01 4/02/01

Approx. size of Earth →

March 30, 2001

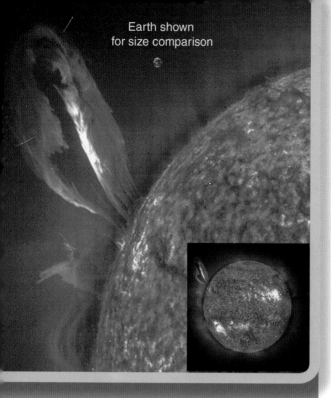
Earth shown for size comparison

The Sun releases powerful bursts of energy that are many times larger than Earth. When these eruptive prominences are directed toward Earth, they can affect communications and power.

Of course, the Sun is always busy producing heat and light. But it also experiences sudden outbursts of energy in the form of **flares** and **coronal mass ejections (CMEs)**. Flares are the most powerful explosions in the entire solar system. They occur near sunspots and release as much energy as a million hydrogen bombs or a billion megatons of TNT. If it could be harnessed, energy from the biggest flares could provide enough electrical power to power the United States for about 100,000 years.

Coronal mass ejections are massive eruptions of plasma from the Sun's corona. Flares and CMEs, along with the solar wind, create what scientists call **space weather**. As the Sun approaches the maximum phase of the solar cycle, space weather becomes more dramatic. This increase in solar activity also affects conditions on Earth. Blasts of highly charged protons and electrons from the Sun can cause power blackouts or dangerous power surges, disrupt communication networks, and even endanger the lives of astronauts. Violent space weather during a solar maximum can also impact such everyday activities as talking on a cell phone or using an ATM machine.

Scientists think a new eleven-year solar cycle is underway. In January 2008 the cycle's first sunspot appeared. The appearance of this sunspot is a sign of what is coming. We can now expect a gradual increase in the number of sunspots and solar storms, and an increasing risk to the electrical systems we depend on. The new cycle, called Solar Cycle 24, will probably reach its peak, or solar maximum, in 2011 or 2012. Between now and then, we could be in for some pretty rough weather—space weather, that is.

This coronal mass ejection was photographed in 2002. The powerful blast released billions of tons of particles into outer space. These particles were traveling at speeds that were more than a million miles per hour.

4

EARTH-SUN CONNECTIONS

Without the Sun, Earth would be a big cold rock in space. In fact, if there were no Sun, our solar system would not even exist. The Sun makes life possible.

THE NEED FOR LIGHT AND HEAT

Photosynthesis is one of the most important interactions between the Sun and Earth. Through this process, the leaves of green plants absorb sunlight to change carbon dioxide and water into simple sugars. These sugars provide energy for the plants, which are the only living things that make their own

Nearly all living organisms—especially plants—require sunlight to grow and survive.

food. Obviously, we humans cannot eat sunshine directly, but we can eat parts of the plants in which the Sun's energy is stored as food.

Plants also absorb carbon dioxide from the atmosphere and release oxygen by the process of photosynthesis. This exchange of gases depends on sunlight and is essential to the health of the planet. We need oxygen in order to breathe. We also need to control the amount of carbon dioxide in the atmosphere, and plants play an important role in that.

Each time we switch on a light in our home or turn up the thermostat when we are cold, we are using electricity. In the United States, more than half of the electricity we use comes from burning coal, which is a fossil fuel. Coal is what becomes of plants that lived millions of years ago. Those plants, like plants today, depended on sunlight in order to live. When we burn coal in power plants, we are releasing the energy of ancient sunlight.

Scientists have also found ways to harness the Sun's rays to create power. Thanks to solar panels, it is now possible to tap the Sun's energy directly without

The energy stored in coal and other fossil fuels came from sunlight that was absorbed nearly a million years ago.

Solar panels harness the power of the Sun to make usable energy. These panels are even used on the International Space Station to generate power and heat.

burning fossil fuels. As a source of non-polluting power, solar panels use specially designed cells to convert sunlight into electricity. Although the development of solar energy is still in an early stage, its use is growing. Even the Hubble Space Telescope uses solar panels for part of its electricity.

Sunlight also causes water from lakes and oceans to evaporate. What do you think happens when water vapor in the atmosphere begins to cool? It falls as rain or snow. Rainwater and melting snow replenish our reservoirs so we have enough water to drink. Plants and animals need water, too, in order to live and grow.

The planet also needs wind. Wind helps plants and other organisms reproduce by spreading seeds and spores, and helps to cool hot areas so that living things can survive. When you fly a kite, ride a wave in the ocean, or sail a boat, you are depending on the wind. Wind gets its start from the Sun. Sunlight heats the

From fun activities, such as flying a kite, to more necessary ones, such as cooling scorching temperatures, wind is a vital part of life on Earth.

air. Warm air rises and when it does, cooler air moves in to take its place. This movement of air is what we call the wind. But without the Sun's influence, the wind would not blow.

THE SEASONS

It takes Earth one year to make a complete orbit around the Sun. The distance between the Earth and the Sun changes slightly during the year. But this difference is not what causes the seasons to change. We have different seasons because of how much light Earth receives from the Sun at different times of the year.

Earth is always leaning in the same direction as it orbits the Sun. Because the tilt is always in the same direction, sunlight hits the Earth at different angles as Earth orbits the Sun. When the Northern Hemisphere is leaning away from the Sun, the northern half of the planet receives less direct light than the southern part. So the days grow shorter and colder as autumn turns into winter. When the Northern Hemisphere is tilted toward the Sun,

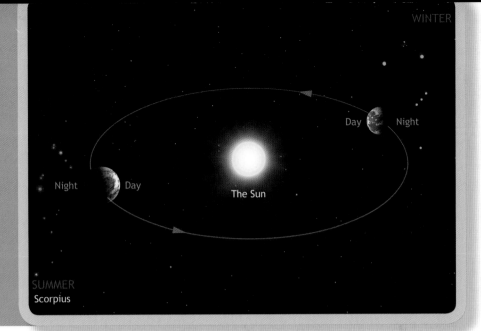

Day and night occur as Earth rotates on its axis, while the planet's orbit around the Sun gives rise to the seasons.

WINTER

Day Night

Night Day

The Sun

SUMMER
Scorpius

the situation is reversed. Now the days grow longer and hotter as spring becomes summer. Spring and summer are warmer than the autumn and winter because sunlight falls on the Earth at a more direct angle during those seasons. The seasons in the two halves of the globe, or hemispheres, are opposite from each other. When one half is having winter, the other half is having summer.

SUNRISE AND SUNSET

It takes Earth a year to orbit around the Sun, but the planet makes a full rotation on its axis (an imaginary line going through the center) in twenty-four hours. Within this time period, the Sun seems to rise and set. This is because the Earth is spinning on its axis from west to east. As a result, in most places for most of the year, the Sun rises in the east and sets in the west.

47

RAINBOWS AND AURORAS

Have you ever seen a rainbow in the sky? Rainbows are a beautiful expression of the Sun's never-ending connection with Earth. When the ancient Greeks looked at rainbows, they thought of a goddess named Iris. Rainbows to them were a sign of her presence and her beauty. But we now know that rainbows are what happen when sunlight passes through drops of water at just the right angle. The water droplets act like glass prisms. They refract and reflect sunlight, breaking it apart into a spectrum of colors from red to violet.

Auroras are an even more stunning example of the Sun's interaction with Earth. These shimmering curtains of light occur in both hemispheres. In the north, they are called the aurora borealis, or the northern lights. In the south, they are called the aurora australis, or the southern lights. Charged particles cause oxygen and nitrogen gases to glow. Scientists concluded that some high-speed collisions between

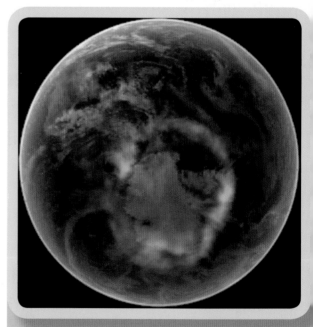

From space, auroras look like glowing rings of light that surround Earth's poles.

48

The northern lights are colorfully displayed in the sky above this home in Alaska.

gases in Earth's atmosphere and incoming electrons are what create auroras. Until recently, scientists thought these electrons came from the Sun.

Satellite transmissions paint a different picture of how auroras form. It now appears that powerful storms on the Sun can cause electrical currents to form in Earth's magnetic field. When this flow of charged particles enters the upper atmosphere, atoms of oxygen and nitrogen light up. On Earth we see this effect as the dazzling colors of an aurora.

49

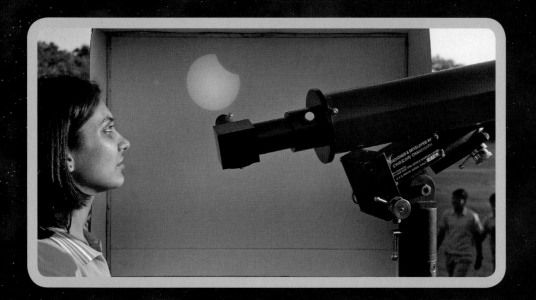

SAFELY VIEWING THE SUN

Because its rays are so strong, you should never look directly at the Sun. Radiation from the Sun can cause severe eye damage. Using projection is the safest way to view the Sun. One projection method requires a telescope or binoculars (with one lens covered), a piece of white paper or poster board, and an easel or chair to hold the paper or poster board. Without looking through it, position the telescope or binoculars so that it faces the Sun. Place the paper or poster board a short distance from the eyepiece of the telescope or binoculars. Adjust the telescope or binoculars until an image of the Sun is projected onto the paper or poster board. Remember that you must NEVER look through the eyepiece or put your hand between the paper and the lens of the telescope or binoculars. The Sun's radiation can cause bad burns in a very short period of time.

MAGNETIC FIELDS AND STORMS

If you take an ordinary magnet and put it under a piece of paper, and then sprinkle iron filings on top of the paper, what happens? The filings arrange themselves in a pattern around the magnet. They are lining up along invisible lines called magnetic field lines.

Earth is like a giant magnet with invisible magnetic field lines. These lines form what scientists call the magnetosphere. The magnetosphere shields the Earth from the solar wind. Without this shield, the solar wind would flood the Earth with

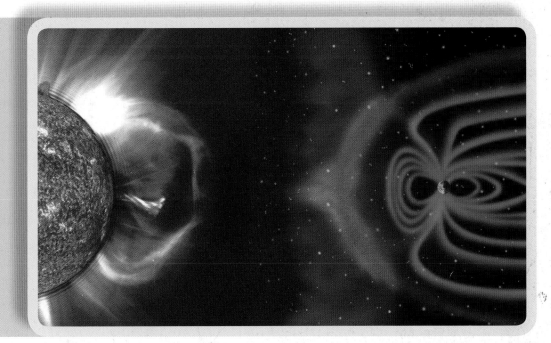

Earth's magnetic field (shown here in blue) protects the planet from the powerful solar winds.

51

charged particles, which can do a lot of damage to satellites and electrical systems. The solar wind is so strong it actually warps, or changes, the shape of the magnetosphere. It compresses the side facing the Sun and stretches the opposite side. If it were visible, the side facing away would look like a long tail streaming for thousands of miles into space.

The Sun has a magnetic field, too. But it is twice as strong as Earth's. Astronomers think the force of magnetism may be responsible for most of what happens on the Sun. Sunspots, solar flares, and coronal mass ejections, for example, are probably the results of changes in the Sun's magnetic field and the build up of magnetic energy inside the Sun. When this energy breaks through the Sun's surface, powerful solar storms develop that can trigger **geomagnetic storms** on Earth.

When you think of storms, you might imagine a thunderstorm with driving rain and explosions of lightning. But a geomagnetic storm has nothing to do with rain, wind, or lightning. This kind of storm involves dramatic changes in Earth's magnetic field. It is the result of violent explosions of charged gas on the Sun. One such explosion—or coronal mass ejection—occurred in April 2000. A shock wave from the Sun took only two days to reach the Earth's magnetosphere. The wave was so powerful it triggered glowing red auroras that could be seen as far south as North Carolina and in northern Europe, Canada, and Alaska.

SOLAR SPACE MISSIONS

Astronomers are far from knowing everything there is to know about the Sun. But without space flight, many mysteries would probably remain unsolved. Orbiting space telescopes and satellites are able to look much more deeply into the Sun than Earth-based observatories. In 1957, the former Soviet Union launched *Sputnik 2*. This was the first satellite to study the Sun from outer space. Since then, there has been a series of missions into space to learn more about the Sun—what it is made of, how it creates energy, and how it affects Earth and the rest of the solar system.

After *Sputnik 2*, the United States began its own study of the Sun from space. The Pioneer program, begun in the late 1950s,

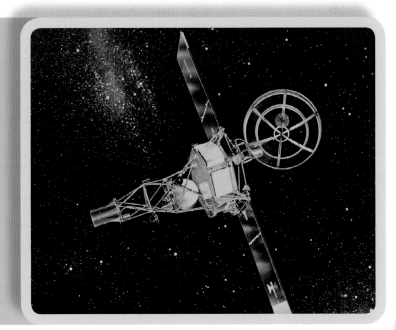

Mariner 2 was the first spacecraft to measure characteristics of solar wind, such as its velocity, density, and composition.

53

included several missions that made important discoveries about the Sun. *Mariner 2*, launched in 1962, revealed that the Sun releases a continuous stream of high-energy particles—the solar wind.

Astronauts aboard the *Skylab* space station, launched in 1973, used X-ray telescopes to study the Sun's corona. In the 1980s, the *Solar Maximum Mission* spacecraft investigated solar flares and other characteristics of the Sun when it is most active.

In the late 1990s and early 2000s, the solar spacecraft *Ulysses* and *SOHO* provided astronomers with vital information about the solar wind and the Sun's magnetic field. Both spacecraft are joint missions of the United States and Europe. *SOHO* stands for *Solar and Heliospheric Observatory*. *SOHO* went into orbit in December 1995. Instruments aboard this satellite have given scientists a new understanding of the Sun's interior and its superheated corona.

For many years, scientists who study the Sun could not explain why the atmosphere is so much hotter than the surface. The corona, the outermost layer of the Sun's atmosphere, is more than one hundred times hotter than

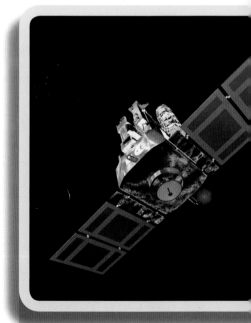

According to NASA data, *SOHO* weighs approximately 2 tons (1.8 tonnes) and has solar panels that make it nearly 25 feet (7.6 m) across

54

the surface. Where is the energy coming from to cause this huge hike in temperature? In 1997 new findings from the *SOHO* spacecraft may have solved the mystery. The satellite's instruments measured magnetic energy rising from the Sun's surface toward the corona. Scientists concluded that the amount of this energy is enough to heat the corona to temperatures higher than 1 million degrees Fahrenheit

HESSI was launched into space on February 5, 2002. This spacecraft's main purpose is to gather data related to the energy release by solar flares.

(555,538 million degrees C). According to a scientist working on the project, *SOHO* is "the most important spacecraft in the history of solar physics."

Looking ahead, the European Space Agency plans to launch the *Solar Orbiter* satellite around 2015. This spacecraft will travel closer to the Sun than any previous solar mission. It will be part of the International Living With a Star program. The program brings together scientists from all over the world who want to study the Sun and its relationship with Earth and the other planets in our solar system.

55

RED GIANT, WHITE DWARF, BOILING SEAS

When we step outside on a warm, sunny day, it is hard to believe there was once a time when there was no Sun. Our Sun is now about halfway through its life. It has enough hydrogen fuel to go on shining for at least another 4.5 billion years. But what will happen when most of the hydrogen has been used up? By studying stars in other parts of our galaxy, scientists have a pretty good idea about how our Sun will spend its final days.

Once the hydrogen fuel in the Sun's core is gone, the Sun will begin to swell until it becomes a **red giant**, one hundred times larger than its present size. By then, the Sun's scorching outer atmosphere will spread past Mercury and Venus and possibly even as far as Earth. Oceans on Earth will boil and evaporate. The land will flow like molten lava. Life will no longer exist.

Temperatures in the Sun's core will become so extreme that any remaining helium will fuse into carbon. Over the next hundred thousand years, the Sun will cast off the outer layers of its atmosphere into space. Scientists do not know for sure what will happen next. One likely scenario is that the outer layers may form colorful rings of gas called a planetary nebula. This glowing cloud might eventually spread to the far reaches of our solar system.

All that will remain of the Sun will be a white dwarf in the center of an expanding gas shell. This white dwarf star will be about the size of Earth but much more dense. A tiny pinch of material from the white dwarf would weigh about as much as two cars! It will take millions of years for the white dwarf to cool completely.

In the end, what was once our Sun will be a dying light in space that will eventually flicker out for good. But all these changes will not happen for billions of years in the future. It is possible that long before our Sun becomes a red giant, we humans will have left the Earth far behind and learned to live on other worlds where other Suns continue to shine. But until then, we will continue to bask in its rays, use its heat, and depend on its existence for our own.

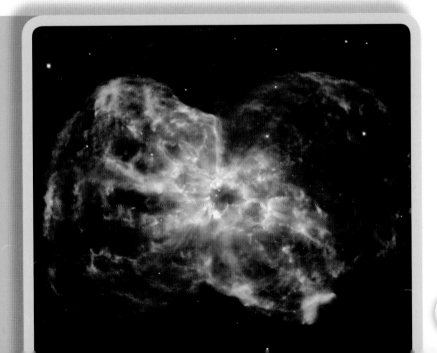

This image from the Hubble Space Telescope shows a Sun-like star as it dies. Scientists predict that our Sun will die in a similar manner more than 4 billion years from now.

57

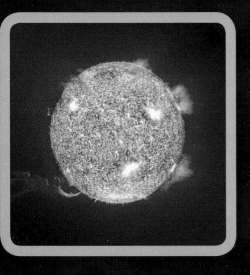

QUICK FACTS ABOUT THE SUN

TYPE OF CELESTIAL BODY: Star

APPROXIMATE AGE: 4.5 billion years

DIAMETER: Approximately 860,000 miles (1.4 million km)

DISTANCE FROM EARTH: Approximately 93 million miles (150 million km)

CHEMICAL MAKEUP: Mostly hydrogen and helium

SURFACE TEMPERATURE: Approximately 10,000 degrees Fahrenheit (5500 degrees C)

INTERIOR TEMPERATURE: At least 28 million degrees Fahrenheit (15.5 million degrees C) at the core

GLOSSARY

astronomer—A scientist who studies planets, stars, and galaxies.

aurora—A colorful display of electrically charged gases in Earth's atmosphere.

black hole—An invisible object in outer space formed when a massive star collapses from its own gravity. The gravitational force of a black hole is so strong that not even light can escape from it.

chromosphere—The reddish layer of the Sun's atmosphere directly above the surface and only visible during a solar eclipse.

convection—The transfer of heat energy by the movement of currents in the Sun's interior.

corona—The hottest and outermost layer of the Sun's atmosphere.

coronal mass ejection (CME) —A massive and very powerful eruption of hot gases from the Sun's atmosphere.

cosmic microwave background radiation (CMB)—The cosmic afterglow of the Big Bang, which happened more than 13 billion years ago.

elementary particles—Extremely tiny forms of matter found inside an atom. The most common forms of elementary particles are protons, neutrons, and electrons.

flares—Extremely powerful explosions of energy in the Sun's atmosphere.

geomagnetic storm—A disturbance in Earth's magnetic field caused by violent eruptions of charged gas on the Sun.

gravity—The force between objects that makes them attract each other. The force of gravity increases as objects come closer together and decreases the farther apart they are.

luminosity—The measure of a star's brightness.

microwaves—A form of radiation or light energy not visible to human eyes.

nebula—An immense cloud of dust and gas molecules in outer space.

photosphere—The surface of the Sun visible from Earth.

radiation—The release of energy in the form of light waves.

red giant—A super-enlarged star that has burned up most of its hydrogen fuel and become many times brighter than it had been.

satellite—A celestial body that orbits around a planet or star—can be natural or human-made. For example, the Moon is one of Earth's natural satellites, while astronomers can launch mechanical satellites that transmit information back to Earth.

solar core—The center of the Sun in which hydrogen is converted to helium and energy through nuclear fusion.

solar wind—A steady stream of gas particles from the Sun's atmosphere.

space weather—Changes in Earth's magnetic field caused by the solar wind and violent eruptions on the Sun in the form of flares or coronal mass ejections.

spiral galaxy—A type of galaxy with arms that spiral outward from the center and which contain many young stars, making the arms brighter and more visible than the center, or nucleus.

sunspots—Dark areas on the surface of the Sun that are cooler than the surrounding area.

supernova—The explosion of a star causing it to become much brighter than it had been.

vacuum—A space in which there is no air or gas. Outer space is a vacuum.

white dwarf—A very small, dense star that has collapsed on itself.

FIND OUT MORE

BOOKS

Chrismer, Melanie. *The Sun*. New York: Children's Press, 2008.

Crosswell, Ken. *Ten Worlds: Everything that Orbits the Sun.* Honesdale, PA: Boyds Mills Press, 2006.

Elkins-Tanton, Linda T. *The Sun, Mercury, and Venus.* New York: Chelsea House, 2006.

Winrich, Ralph. *The Sun*. Mankato, Minn: Capstone Press, 2008.

WEBSITES

Astronomy for Kids
http://www.kidsastronomy.com/deep_space.htm

Explore the Sun
http://www.kidscosmos.org/kid-stuff/sun-facts.html

NASA Sun Earth Media Viewer: Live Solar Images
http://sunearth.gsfc.nasa.gov/sunearthday/media_viewer/flash.html

The Nine Planets Solar System Tour
http://seds.lpl.arizona.edu/nineplanets/nineplanets

StarChild: A Learning Center for Young Astronomers
http://starchild.gsfc.nasa.gov/docs/StarChild/StarChild.html

Sun for Kids
http://www.nasa.gov/vision/universe/solarsystem/sun_for_kids_main.html

The Virtual Sun
http://www.astro.uva.nl/dcmo/Sun/kaft.htm

Windows to the Universe
http://www.windows.ucar.edu/windows.html

BIBLIOGRAPHY

The author found these resources especially helpful when researching this book.

The Astronomical Institute of the University of Amsterdam. "The Virtual Sun." http://www.astro.uva.nl/demo/sun/home.htm

Exploratorium. "Solar Eclipse." http://www.exploratorium.edu/eclipse/cmes5.html

Hartmann, William K. and Ron Miller. *The Grand Tour: A Traveler's Guide to the Solar System*. New York: Workman Publishing Company, 2005.

HubbleSite. "Hubble's Deepest View Ever of the Universe Unveils Earliest Galaxies." http://hubblesite.org/newscenter/archive/releases/2004/07/

HyperPhysics—Georgia State University. "Galaxies." http://hyperphysics.phy-astr.gsu.edu/Hbase/astro/galax.html

NASA. "SOHO." http://soho.nascom.nasa.gov/about/about.html

National Geographic. "Sun." http://science.nationalgeographic.com/science/space/solar-system/sun-article.html

---. "A Reason for the the Season." http://www.nationalgeographic.com/xpeditions/activities/07/season.html

Odenwald, Sten. "Living with a Star." http://ds9.ssl.berkeley.edu/lws_gems/6/secef_6.htm

Science Encyclopedia. "Sun: A Brief History of Solar Observations." http://science.jrank.org/pages/6603/Sun-brief-history-solar-observations.html

Shestople, Paul. "Big Bang Cosmology Primer." http://cosmology.berkeley.edu/Education/IUP/Big_Bang_Primer.html

Stanford Solar Center. "The Singing Sun." http://solar-center.stanford.edu/singing/singing.html

INDEX

63

ABOUT THE AUTHOR

George Capaccio is both a writer and a storyteller. He loves to visit schools and perform stories from all over the world. He also enjoys writing educational books about history and science. He lives in Arlington, Massachusetts, with his wife, Nancy, and their Golden Retriever.